WRITING
FOR
MAGAZINES

THE ESSENTIAL GUIDE

Need
— 2 —
Know

Writing for Magazines – The Essential Guide is also available in accessible formats for people with any degree of visual impairment. The large print edition and eBook (with accessibility features enabled) are available from Need2Know. Please let us know if there are any special features you require and we will do our best to accommodate your needs.

First published in Great Britain in 2011 by
Need2Know
Remus House
Coltsfoot Drive
Peterborough
PE2 9BF
Telephone 01733 898103
Fax 01733 313524
www.need2knowbooks.co.uk

Contents

Introduction

You love magazines and you'd like to write for them. Perhaps you're a student, or retired with more time to write, or you just have topics and experiences you're longing to put into print. It's never too early or too late to start writing. And you'd love to see your name in a magazine! Yet it can seem a huge challenge to gain entry to such a competitive industry. How to begin?

The good news is – that's just how all magazine writers felt at the start of their writing careers. The first step is always simply gaining the confidence to submit your work. Many writers long to be published in magazines, but are convinced their work isn't 'good enough' to even bother submitting. The world of magazines may seem too daunting to approach.

The confidence to be bold and make a start is acquired much more easily when you're armed with some professional know-how. And that's exactly what this book gives you – it's crammed with practical advice on how to research your market, find ideas, study magazines professionally, craft your copy and submit your work to editors.

There are suggestions on magazine openings that could be right for you, with step-by-step help on marketing yourself and your work. Advice on preparing your work professionally – and even on how to talk successfully to an editor – is included. One of the most vital chapters covers the essential easy-to-do magazine market research that will enhance your chances of success one hundred percent. Despite problems the magazine industry has faced, there are still 8,000 magazines out there . . . they all need words.

Writing for magazines is a bit like being an actor – you've got to expect rejection some of the time. Rejection can be tough. It can feel as if it's you, not your writing, that's being turned down. But you'll learn from this book that with ways of handling it, rejection will not crush your writing or your spirit. You'll be able to pick yourself up and start again, quickly. An article of yours, sent back by one magazine may, with some tweaks, be just right for another one.

Another problem with would-be – and even professional! – magazine writers can be concentration, so time management and focus is covered here. There are tips on setting up a pleasant and productive writing space and avoiding those ever-present time-wasting distractions. With this book, you'll always enjoy your work.

When you've read it, you'll also be at home with some technical terms used by magazine editors dealing with your articles. These are easily explained and not hard to follow. It's a definite asset to know them. You'll be able to understand some basic legal issues like libel and copyright too.

It's good to aim high as a magazine writer. With the professional insider advice this book will give you, you'll be head and shoulders above the competition when it comes to being noticed by editors.

Good luck and happy magazine writing!

Chapter One

Take That First Step

How to start? There are more than 8,000 print magazines out there. And they all need writers. Your goal is to break into those markets. It does mean that, for now, you will most likely join the hopefuls – the 'unsoliciteds'. You'll be a freelance writer trying to market ideas and articles to editors.

Remember that small and niche magazines in particular rely heavily on freelance contributions. And the more professional skills you acquire, the more you increase your chances of success. It can be a question of persistence as well as talent – the first step is the hardest. Anxiety can be your opponent here. Anxiety can prevent you even starting to put words onto your screen.

When I started my career as a newspaper reporter, at the age of 16, beginning an article was always a tense time. Where to start? How to grab the reader's attention? How to say it best – and when to finish? I'd stare at the typewriter (yes – typewriter), jot down notes but be almost afraid of letting go and writing.

And that's what you have to do: let go. Tidying your desk, setting out your pens and notebooks, making cups of coffee all have their place – but they can be used as displacement activities. I've sometimes made three cups of hot chocolate and eaten two packets of crisps before I started pounding the keyboard. I had a feeling I had to be comfortable before I could start writing.

Wrong! Have you said that – or thought it? We often adopt a 'stand and deliver' attitude to life – we'll be happy when this, this and the other (a new job, a new relationship, a new house) happens – and not a minute before!

'There are more than 8,000 magazines out there. And they all need writers.'

Four skills

You need four things to be a magazine writer – an idea, a market, creative talent and an eye for business. But before all those, you need confidence. It's easy for your confidence to take a back seat, for you to sabotage your peace of mind with worries, fears, panics, fretting.

You begin to doubt that anything you write is worthwhile. You begin to be nervous about putting words on the page. You begin to feel that you don't deserve to be a writer. That nothing you write will ever be published. You can't imagine submitting anything, because you are sure it will be rejected. And so it goes on . . . and on . . . and on . . .

The ability to be comfortable with things as they are is an essential quality for your writing. It's really about developing a kind of flexibility. And the more flexible you can be, the easier it is to cope with whatever life throws at you. And the easier it is to write!

Getting the confidence to write

Confidence comes from having plans and goals written down. Don't just plunge in, but fill in this 5-point plan – in writing!

The 5-point plan

- The most important decisions to make are – what kind of magazines will you aim for? Thinking this through will help your confidence.

- What do I want from my writing career?

- What do I have to offer?

- Who might buy what I have to offer?

- How do I reach the people who want to buy what I have to offer?

Magazines you could write for could be:

- Women's magazines, from *Take a Break* to *The Lady*

- Niche magazines – magazines about pets, food, caravans and hundreds more hobbies and interests.

- Magazines included with Sunday and Saturday newspapers.

- Trade magazines – if you have insider and specialist knowledge of anything from insurance to cars.

- Travel magazines.

- Local city and county magazines.

You'll need to do research on your chosen field, and there's more on this in chapter two. You can identify the kind of magazine you'd like to write for, and what kind of material they want.

My passion has always been for women's magazines, but I've also been managing editor of a consumer magazine for Iceland frozen foods, a magazine about cross-stitch, and a glossy travel magazine. I have also written many features for the *Sunday Mirror* magazine, *The Lady*, and features for county and city magazines.

I began my career in newspapers, as women's editor (newspaper women's pages are really mini magazines) then switched to glossy magazines. I love them! But in the beginning my confidence wasn't high. In every case, the first time I wrote for a new market – like the *Sunday Mirror* magazine – I was almost traumatised by the challenge of starting. I had to force myself, I was so afraid of not being 'good enough'.

Yet, once I'd had work accepted, then new work commissioned, I relaxed. The more you write, the more you can write. Aim to be productive – not perfect – when you write. Polish and hone your writing later. Get the words onto the screen and build them up!

Yes to Yearbook

Your bible is the latest copy of *The Writers' and Artists' Yearbook* (A&C Black). It lists every magazine in the UK, Australia and Canada, giving an idea of their requirements and contact details.

I can't stress too much how vital it is to target your work to the right magazine. If you want to write family features, you wouldn't be sending your work to finance publications; if you have a yen for local history articles, teenage magazines would not be very profitable markets. It sounds obvious, but you'd be surprised how inappropriate some articles are when sent to an editor. But not from you – the Yearbook can be your guide!

Setting up your writing space

Having said that too much titivating can be a displacement activity, it is still important to set up a dedicated writing space. It doesn't matter how small it is, as long as it's neat, and you have all you need to work. I've worked in the hallway of a two-room flat, in my bedroom, and kitchen. No matter how tiny the space, as long as it's all yours, you can write.

Essentials

- Laptop or desktop computer.
- Internet access and email.
- Printer and plain copy paper.
- Notebooks and pens.
- Shelves to store books and magazines.
- Folders to store your finished work.
- Scrapbook with clear pages to display your published work – this is your presentation portfolio. You can make an on-line one, too.
- Colour – when you need stationery (Post-its, notebooks, paperclips even postage stamps) go for the most colourful ones, those that please you most. Each time you use that apple-green ring folder or a bright commemorative stamp, you'll feel a small glow of pleasure.
- Small portions of delicious 'treat' food can be a reward for your writing sessions – but get them in advance.

That's the picture of happiness for most of us writers: to enter your own well-organised workspace – no matter how small; to know you don't have to go out for errands; that you have a few hours ahead of you just for your writing and a new book to read in the evening. Away you go – with optimism.

Three tricks for aiding the writer in you:

- Buy flowers – just a splash of colour will lift your spirits. Arrange them where you can see them – maybe on your desk?

- Keep your living and working space tidy and fresh – no need to be obsessive. Chuck out wastepaper every day. Arrange your paperbacks in colour-coded order – put all those vintage orange Penguins together.

- Plot your writing sessions – maybe from 10 to 12, or 2 to 4? At the allotted time, you turn up at your computer!

Multitasking doesn't work when you're writing. Focus on one project at a time, one idea, one goal. Punctuating your work with trips to do laundry, or chats with friends, Facebook updates, or working out your budget, or worrying about your bank balance – this dilutes your concentration.

Your writing brain responds to focusing on one thing and one thing only. As you work steadily on, it becomes easier – maybe almost effortless – and you're 'in the flow'. That's an ideal state; you're lost to the world! It's just you and your writing – perfect.

Write about what you know

Writing from your own experience works for both articles and short stories for magazines – though of course you add imagination to the short stories.

Group your interests into work experience, hobbies and personal: jot them down. These interests are the raw material for your magazine articles.

Writing about what you know is key to successful magazine article writing, and also helpful in short stories. If you've worked in an office, backpacked through Thailand, done a course in how to make cupcakes – you've got material.

'Writing about what you know is key to successful magazine article writing, and also helpful in short stories. If you've worked in an office, backpacked through Thailand, done a course in how to make cupcakes – you've got material.'

It might be your hobby you could write about – sailing, cycling, cooking Indian food, patchwork. Or it could be a life stage you are going through – a gap year, first-time motherhood, starting work for the first time.

All experiences can be material – and they don't all have to be 'good' experiences. For example, there's a market in writing about being jobless, or job-hunting, or coping with an illness.

These are all topics with which millions of readers identify. If you have experience in certain fields – let's say finance, teaching, catering – you could find markets in professional magazines. The writing skills for niche magazines are just the same as for consumer publications.

Simple structure

There's more on the practicals of writing in chapter 4, but I want to give you some examples now of how you can use, let's say, your work experience for your articles.

For a magazine feature

Pick one incident from your work now, or a job you've had before, and begin there. A first person piece could work well. Make it amusing, maybe add some tips on the job which you learned while doing it.

For example, while working in the office of a hypnotherapist, I picked up some conversational techniques that have helped me defuse potentially difficult 'complaint' exchanges in shops and restaurants. A word count of 750 to 1,250 is enough. Don't name the company unless you know they won't object. Change a few key details such as location.

'All experiences can be material – and they don't all have to be 'good' ones. For example, there's a market in writing about being jobless, or job-hunting, or coping with an illness.'

Need2Know

For a short story

The possibilities are huge. It's just a question of setting your short story in a work environment. Editors of women's magazines complain they don't get enough work-based short stories – so this is your opportunity. Most short stories centre on domestic settings and relationships. Your story will stand out because editors are starved of fiction that is set in and around the workplace.

For a reader's letter

Pick out an opinion you have about work. For example, should music be played in offices and factories? Make it short and lively! Reader's letters are often a start to a magazine writing career – they were for me. There's more on this later.

Begin with a piece of writing you know you'll enjoy – not a tricky part. Start in the middle of, or even at the end of, a feature or story. Then when you've got your brain in gear, you can begin to hone and shape the rest of your piece.

Leave things at an 'incomplete' turn – maybe even in the middle of a sentence – so that the next day you're ready to go. It's a lot easier to start writing again if you don't have to think about where to begin.

The importance of a professional approach to your work

Sunrise scribe

The early hours are very, very productive. If you've been feeling low or depressed, maybe not working at a regular office job, it's possible you've slid into get-up-late mode. Without a working structure, many of us do this.

Yet, if you can start the habit, the energy that comes from getting up early is surprising – it can last all day. Plus, you'll be able to fit in chores and tasks, and a day job. You don't even have to get dressed to write. But you do have to be warm – so comfort clothes are called for.

Here's what a student of mine wrote after starting an 'early morning writing' routine.

'I found myself up at 7am, the sun pouring in through my window, sitting at my desk with a large cup of coffee at my elbow. My computer was on and I was making notes for my short story – bliss! I live alone, am not working at the moment, and sometimes am lethargic about getting up. But when I realised that this freedom actually gave me the freedom to organise my time well – not in a haphazard way – I began to relish it. When I'm up that early, it's fine to go to bed early or even have a nap in the afternoon! But the joy of being so productive almost at dawn stays with me all day. It really works.'

Career progress

As a freelance magazine writer, it's up to you to develop your own career. No employer provides free training or workshops. But you can do this yourself with ease by:

Going to a bookshop talk

Don't just think about attending a reading at a local bookshop – buy the ticket now! Here's a chance to be very happy for a few hours, and longer, as you reflect on the evening afterwards and maybe even buy the speaker's book. Best-selling authors can be heard for just a few pounds; some are even free. Buy tickets only for speakers you'd really love to hear.

Attending a literary festival

Every major city in the UK has a literary festival with a raft of talks, workshops and seminars – tickets are inexpensive, and there are concessions. Pick events that will make you happy . . .

Attend a course

Ask for Christmas or birthday cash towards a writing course holiday. Arvon is one of the most respected, but there are courses abroad, too (see help list).

Buy a notebook and use it

Write down snippets of dialogue, thoughts that occur, observations, ideas and plots. Write them down as they come to you. You can use your notebook anywhere – in a café, on the bus, in a hospital waiting room. Your notebook is essential – unless you write your thoughts down, shape them, you're only daydreaming!

Fill notebooks

Try to fill up your notebook in a month – as recommended by Natalie Goldberg in *Writing Down the Bones* (Shambhala.) Choose your notebook carefully – make sure the size makes your plan achievable. Ryman's, WHSmith or supermarkets are fine for good but inexpensive notebooks. Don't spend a lot on something with a moleskin cover.

Dialogue doodles

Here's something you can begin in your notebook today. Jot down one snatch of dialogue a day – from life. You don't even have to think of an idea – just listen to other people . . . eavesdrop. It's free, it's fun . . . and it's legal. You'll find it very rewarding. Writing from life, it can be almost a diary.

'Write down those snippets of dialogue, thoughts that occur, observations, ideas and plots. Write them down as they happen. You can use your notebook anywhere – in a café, on the bus, in a hospital waiting room, anywhere.'

Summing Up

- Buy a writing notebook – essential!
- Think hard about which magazines you want to write for.
- Create a neat writing space.
- Begin to jot down some dialogue snippets – if you can manage one a day, that's great.
- All writers lack confidence in 'starting' articles and short stories.
- Aim to be productive, not perfect, when you begin to write.
- Early hours can be very productive!

Chapter Two

Market Research

What do you want to write about?

When you aim to break into magazine writing, you'll almost certainly join the large and ever-growing army of freelancers pitching their ideas and articles to editors. How can you improve your chances of success?

You should never sit down and write an article without knowing exactly which magazine you'll be aiming it at. Careful market research is vital. Targeting your work at magazines and meeting the needs of their readers is crucial. The professional way to find out what editors want is to do your market research before you write your articles.

How to start

Begin by simply listing some topics you could write about. These could be your opinions about matters of topical or general interest – known as 'think pieces'. They could be personal experiences, travel reports, interviews, or articles based on your specialist knowledge.

Next, find out what's on the news stands in newsagents and supermarkets. Research on the Internet to find magazines in your sphere of interest. Every title has an online presence. The Internet version enhances the important club feel of every magazine: many of them run reader clubs, too. This club feel is the number one ingredient in a magazine's success.

'You should never sit down and write an article without knowing exactly which magazine you'll be aiming it at. Careful market research is vital. Targeting your work at any magazine, and meeting the needs of its readers, is crucial.'

Readers collect magazines and write to them (or for them!) and are part of their 'family'. Every magazine reader is part of a group or community. It could be a community of students, young mums, computer game fans, keen cooks . . . and hundreds more. It's a club.

What do magazines offer?

'Readers collect magazines, write to them (or for them!) and are part of their "family". Every magazine reader is part of a group or community. It could be a community of students, young mums, computer game fans, keen cooks . . . and hundreds more.'

Whoever the club is for, there are certain elements in every magazine that it's useful for you to know about for your market research:

▪ The 'me' factor – the reader must look forward to getting the magazine or newsletter, confident that there will be something just right for them in it.

▪ Information the reader can use – contact numbers, helplines, pointers readers can use to improve their lives.

▪ Encouragement in a hobby or interest – which could be local history, gardening, parenting, cooking, travel, and many more.

▪ Inspiration – every magazine or newsletter needs to have a 'feel-good' bonus. This could be as simple as tips for dealing with a student budget, or the dates of three open air rock concerts. It's information the reader can use.

▪ How-to – readers of some magazines want a feeling that new skills can be gained. In a practical gardening magazine, this could be as basic as how to pot up a container; in a food or student magazine, how to dish up supper for four for a fiver. The how-to might mean old skills refreshed or updated, and conveyed in a new way. It doesn't have to be an original activity – though of course it could be.

Join the club

When you identify your own interests and match them to the magazines in these fields, you've taken a big step towards publication.

Let's say, for example, that you want to write about bringing up your child – titles such as *Practical Parenting* will be your best market, since they specialise in features on bringing up young children. But there will be 'secondary' markets, too – magazines such as *Good Housekeeping* or *Woman's Own* which also publish features about bringing up children.

> ### Top tip
>
> You can write for markets which *specialise* in or *include* your subject. That way, you can sell your work more than once . . . recycle it. More on this in a later chapter.

There are also free local magazines which could be markets for you. Other possible outlets are magazines given away by airlines and banks, trade magazines, business magazines and special interest or 'niche' consumer magazines.

You'll have your *Writers' & Artists' Yearbook* – look on it as a one-stop professional library of contact details for magazines. But news stands and the Internet will give you plenty of information on 'your' magazines too.

List your markets

You've listed the ideas you can write about. And you've found out the titles of magazines which cover 'your' topics. Now you can start to draw up and plan a list of your main markets – the magazines most likely to use your articles – and perhaps a couple of secondary markets. Your market research begins in earnest!

Research technique

Plan time for your market research and make notes as you go. Look on your research as a pleasure, keep notes in a special notebook – it's an enjoyable activity, so don't rush it. Time spent on research will reward you later with successful submissions. You'll need to study a few recent copies of each magazine, either online or in print. Magazines do sometimes change their style, so it's important to look at recent issues. Study the magazines carefully, looking at both the articles and at the advertisements.

Articles and ads – why both?

Market research isn't just looking at the editorial content of the magazines. It's about the advertisements as well. These are a vital window into the heart of the magazine.

Are the ads for stairlifts and care homes? For cosmetic surgery and expensive face creams? Lots of mature dating ads and nostalgia music, or for the very latest in personal IT toys? Ads for kids' yogurts and prams, or for fine wines and foods?

From the advertisements, you'll glean an idea of the trends and topics that interest readers of this particular magazine – and you'll be able to gear your language more closely to its readers. You'll see whether your reader is a mum living on a lean budget, a young fashion-conscious woman with income to spend on Chanel perfumes and make up, or someone at or near retirement age interested in nostalgia articles, comfortable clothes, leisurely travel . . . and stairlifts!

'Market research isn't just looking at the editorial content of the magazines. It's about the advertisements as well. These are a vital window into the heart of the magazine.'

Reader profile

Make two lists in your notebook for each magazine you study.

Head one list 'articles' and the other 'ads'. You're noting down the topics of the articles, and the products that are advertised.

From this combination – articles and ads – you can get a rough idea of the typical reader.

Are the articles on topics such as family history and WW2, with advertisements for care homes and pensions? Your reader will be older, perhaps living on a fixed income with not much spare cash for luxuries.

If the features are about age-reducing face creams and relaxation techniques, with ads for cosmetic surgery and spa hotels, your reader is a mature woman with spending power.

However, there will be subjects that cut across all magazines – for example, interviews with celebrities, how to reduce stress, and food features. But for different magazines the approach will be different – *Vogue* and *Woman's Own* may both have interviews with George Clooney, but the angle will be different: the *Woman's Own* one will be much more cosy!

Clues

Several magazines may cover the same subject– for example women's magazines might at first glance seem similar, but there are clues to their individual approaches. These are:

The front cover – often this will be a 'people' picture – you'll be able to tell a lot from this. Teenagers, a celebrity, a mum-type picture, glossy and glamorous, sporty, related to a hobby such as sewing or food?

Advertisements – as we've said, these give you major windows into the reader's profile.

Tone of the content . . . this means the way the words are used.

Watch your tone!

This is another clue in the market research toolbox you're building up. Understanding the tone of the magazine – the way the words in the articles are used – will help in your professional approach as a writer. And it's not hard to do.

You are planning your article for a certain magazine – let's say it's a women's or a travel magazine. Read it for tone – it sounds difficult, but it isn't. All you need to do is begin by reading one piece repeatedly.

Is the style friendly, bossy, self-effacing, serious or neutral? Is it gushing, ironic, nostalgic, cosy, distanced, youthful or jokey? Magazines make a great fuss about 'tone' – it has to be exactly right. For example, if you used *The Sun's* tone for an article you hope to place in *The Times*, you would not get very far. It's just the same with magazines. You couldn't place an article written in *Yours'* style in *Vogue*.

Check that tone

Here's a research checklist for magazine tone.

Is the tone of the magazine you want to write for:

▓ Chatty and friendly . . . older reader magazines such as *Choice* and *Yours*.

▓ Slightly bossy . . . magazines such as *Prima*.

▓ Instructive and neutral – travel and food magazines often adopt this tone.

▓ Full of case histories and 'confessions' written in the first person, starting with 'I' . . . these will be in women's weekly magazines, slimming and health magazines, Sunday and Saturday magazines that are packaged with newspapers.

Follow that style

Are the sentences short and punchy? Does the magazine use short paragraphs and short words, or longer paragraphs with longer words? When you research this and keep a note, it gives you another advantage when you write your own pieces. All you have to do is follow the style they use – it's a simple trick of the trade.

Reader pen picture

You've studied the articles – and the advertisements. You've looked at the style, the tone and the club feel of the magazine. Now you can almost picture your reader.

Draw up a pen picture of the typical reader – why do you think they buy the magazine? What's their likely age range? Are they affluent (readers of *Vogue* and *Red*) or living on more of a budget (women's weeklies such as *Choice* or *Take a Break*)?

Jot down a few adjectives to describe your typical reader. This will help you as a guideline when you start to write your piece. And don't forget – if the magazine is one you love to read yourself, then you are a typical reader too!

Reading both articles and advertisements gives you a huge advantage when you submit your own work. You'll be streets ahead of writers who send off features without bothering to research their markets.

'Draw up a pen picture of the typical reader – why do you think they buy the magazine? What's their likely age range, are they affluent (readers of *Vogue* and *Red*) or living on a budget (women's weeklies such as *Choice* or *Take a Break*)?'

Summing Up

- Think hard about what you can write about for magazines. These will be subjects you know about.

- Invest in *Writers' & Artists' Yearbook*.

- Draw up a list of your possible magazine markets.

- Source magazines – on the news stand and the Internet – which cover your interests.

- Study each copy closely.

- Notice the 'club' feel.

- Look at the advertisements as well as the articles.

- Think about the tone of different magazines.

- Keep notes on all your market research.

Chapter Three

Ideas and Slots for You in Magazines

There are plenty of slots for you in magazines. Any magazine you pick up – from *The Lady* to *My Weekly* – has a spot for you, whether it's a reader's letter, an opinion piece or a short story.

Readers' letters

What makes a good letter?

What's the definition of 'good'?

'From an editor's point of view, the ideal letter is one that requires no editing whatsoever; it's short, grammatically correct and makes its point succinctly. If it's witty, that's a bonus.' *David Kernek, newspaper and travel magazine editor.*

My first letter

The very first time I saw my name in print was when I was nine years old. I wrote a letter to a children's magazine called *Girl* – yes it was a few years ago! And the letter talked about how I had decorated the walls of my attic bedroom with full-page pictures cut out from *Girl* magazine. In every issue they had a beautiful whole-page photograph – anything from a portrait of Audrey Hepburn to a view of a mountain.

'From an editor's point of view, the ideal letter is one that requires no editing whatsoever; it's short, grammatically correct and makes its point succinctly. If it's witty, that's a bonus.'

David Kernek, newspaper and travel magazine editor.

My prize for this seven-line offering was a postal order that would be worth about £10 in today's cash. My joy knew no bounds. But without knowing it, I'd followed exactly the pattern I would recommend to students years later. It's this – for a good chance of your letter being used, always refer to how the magazine has helped you.

Reader's letter checklist

The letter most likely to be used:

- Is short – three or four paragraphs at most.
- Is sent with a picture of the writer.
- Expresses an emotion.
- Is succinct.
- Contains a whole idea.
- Refers to something already printed in the magazine; it might challenge or applaud something that's been published in a recent issue.
- Offers a tip from the writer's experience.
- Shares something that happened to the reader – good or bad.
- Celebrates a personal triumph over tragedy.

'Prizes for readers' letters in women's magazines are excellent. And their letters nearly always refer to a previous issue of the magazine. That's the thing to remember.'

Compliments all round

Prizes for letters in women's magazines are excellent. And their letters nearly always refer to a previous issue of the magazine. That's the thing to remember. So this weekend, as you compose your letter (with your target magazine in front of you), it's good to:

- Compliment the magazine on a recent feature, but go a bit further – include the name of the writer and say what the feature meant to you. Pick out five projects or tips you adopted from the last issue.
- Spotlight a problem or illness that's worrying you, and ask readers for their advice.

▨ Refer to a long-ago issue of the magazine – if you've been collecting the magazine for more than five years – and talk about an idea you still use from it.

Here is a typical 'good' magazine letter:

'Well done Linda Kelsey for going back to university (I Waited 40 Years To Do a Degree, March). I too went back to uni in my 50s. I was teaching full time, going to a Thai boxing class three times a week and a mother of two students – and I graduated just before my 60th birthday. My husband, bless him, scarcely saw me, but it was worth it for that sense of achievement.'

Cathie Corner, Lanarkshire

It's an excellent letter in the May 2011 issue of *Good Housekeeping,* which won the writer a £50 bouquet and the Star Letter slot at the top of the page. The letter is short but contains detail – about the Thai boxing class, her children and her husband's support. You can win a letters' prize by giving details of how an article in the magazine has enhanced your life or reflects your own life. Detail, detail, detail – it's key to winning letters.

Columns and opinion pieces

Columns

Almost every magazine has a slot for an opinion column contributed by readers. Achieving distinction here gives you an excellent cutting.

Columns and opinion pieces are known as 'think' pieces, opinions clearly distinguished from fact.

You can write a think piece in one day. If you are starting out as a writer, it's the simplest to try because:

You need no interviewees – it's your opinion.

You don't have to be an expert to write one. In fact, a viewpoint from a reader, a new name, is often welcome.

'Almost every magazine has a slot for an opinion column contributed by readers. Achieving distinction here gives you an excellent cutting.'

Extensive research is not needed – you can put together an opinion piece based on one accurate fact. Your writing skills are your main tool.

Think pieces are short – they need be no more than 350 words – and certainly no longer than 750 words.

They can be on very uncomplicated topics – issues that might seem trivial yet concern many readers, such as local bus routes savaged by cuts, or how to deal with rude sales assistants.

They're always in demand by magazines. The proliferation of opinion pieces on the Internet websites is chaotic and bewildering – which one to choose?

In many ways, the think piece is the lifeblood of a magazine, just as it was when the printing press was invented. They're the features that generate responses from readers – ensuring that the letters' pages are never empty.

Find your topic

How do you start? The first step is to settle on a subject – pick one that you feel passionate, annoyed, concerned about . . . and would fit into your chosen magazine.

When you write your piece, try writing the opening and final paragraphs first – then filling in the rest of your article. This will aid the structure of your piece.

Rules of play

You've settled on a subject, now:

- Decide what you want to say – what your point is – before you start writing.

- Jot down a 'running order' of your argument before you start to write.

- Make just one point, not 17. You're aiming for a short comment, not a thesis for a degree course!

- If your opinion is based on facts, ensure that you've got the facts right, and attribute their source.

- Be succinct – do not use 10 words if the same work can be done just as well by five.

- Be witty where it's appropriate. Choose the opening words with extra care – these are the words or phrases that will grab the reader's interest, or make them turn the page. Inject some emotion into the first sentence.

Travel

As a novice writer, you are unlikely to be offered a commission to travel to the Seychelles. That might come later! But short, first person articles – taster travel, travel snapshots – are welcomed by magazine editors. It's a slot they might struggle to fill. There may be a small regular section on days out, train travel and budget weekends where an original piece is welcomed.

This could be an entrée into travel writing – my first ever travel piece was on the Wye Valley, a back page piece of 750 words for *Family Circle*. I've also done very short pieces on Beneath Paris (the sightseeing trip into the sewers of Paris) and Bath on a Budget.

Write about yourself and your own experiences, not just a description of the destination. It's your style of writing and your honesty that will make a travel piece swing. It should not read like a guidebook. You could write a travel piece on a day out by bus: a walk around your own town or city: a bookshop or charity shop tour of a city. Include plenty of listings and prices – everything from a cappuccino in a riverside café to a ticket for a tour bus.

Begin with some action

It's always good to begin your short piece at a moment of action . . .

> 'I'm sitting in a space bubble at the Yorvik Viking Centre in York. We're descending further and further back through time – seeing the people, hearing the sounds and even smelling the scents of their era. It's worth every penny of the £9.25 ticket for this strange and inspiring experience. Travelling alone to York for a day out, I also visited four good bookshops, had a delicious vegetarian lunch for £5.95 and later a cream tea with home-made cherry jam (£3.95) in the shadow of the Minster. On foot, it was easy to move between attractions and the endless inviting tea rooms. Warning – don't go during school holidays, as York is also a popular family attraction.'
>
> This is taster travel at its most economic – just 119 words.

You could sum up a place in 500 words. Here's how:

- Pick out three or four details about the destination.
- How to get there.
- Where to stay.
- Where to eat.
- Things to do (a workshop, a class).

In every case, it's always the *detail* – rather than the description – about the destination which will catch an editor's eye. Include phone details, website addresses, costs, discounts, examples of meals, and perhaps a short list highlighting the destination's 'best' and 'worst' aspects.

Interviews

The possibilities for local interviews for national magazines are good. Your interviewee does not have to be famous, though the appetite for celebs is huge. Readers are just as interested in the celeb who gave up stardom. I found a famous 60s pop star – he'd had a few problems – living modestly a street away from my newspaper office, working for a church.

Paint a portrait

The aim of a profile interview is to offer a thoughtful, compelling portrait that does not gloss over any difficulties your subject may have faced.

Happiness is a key. Everyone is fascinated and intrigued by it. Is your subject a happy person? Why is he or she happy – or unhappy? What route to happiness might they recommend to others?

Most people of any distinction – from an award-winning street cleaner to a best-selling author – do have a driving force in their lives, a way of looking at things, a set of values or a theory. That's what you're aiming to grasp, and then convey to your readers.

A magazine profile is not a life story; that's a job for biographers. It is a description of a living person. But the simplest questioning technique is to get your interviewee to cover, briefly, their life – from what they did when they left school or university to now. You can make this less lengthy by requesting a CV or history in bullet points in advance, if that's possible, or finding what's available on the Internet. But don't expect his or her CV, or any Internet website, to be illuminating about your interviewee's character. It's just a guide for your questions, and to avoid having to use interview time for too many functional details.

'A magazine profile is not a life story; that's a job for biographers. It is a description of a living person.'

Just relax

Start your questions with the era of his or her life – or the activity – you think most interests your interviewee. It could be a hobby, war service, music, an art collection – something you know he or she is very involved with. If you are quiet and slightly reserved, but smiling and friendly – you will get your subject on your side.

Have some 'emergency' questions ready for when you fear things are drying up – see overleaf for my list.

Top tip

Use plenty of first person quotes from your interviewee. The written piece should be two-thirds quotes, a third background copy.

Emergency questions:

- Have you a favourite novel/film, piece of music?
- Which books are on your bedside table now?
- If you hadn't become an author/teacher/politician/singer, what might you have been?

Short stories

Your starting point is to study the stories in the magazines. Are they mainly love stories, or do they include the ghost, crime and science fiction genres? Look at the technique of the story – that's important. It could be short with a twist in the tail. Are they all first person stories? Look at the endings – always happy, boy meets girl, boy gets girl? Or are gloomy or complex endings acceptable? Is it triumph over tragedy, good over bad, the 'right' thing winning? Look at characters – young, old, well-off or on modest means?

This will often (but not always) be born out in the settings – council flat, old people's home, or luxury riverside apartment? The settings could be mundane or exotic, perhaps abroad.

Getting an idea of the reader for your short story is exactly the same as the research for your factual magazine articles. It's reader attitudes and interests that are important. Study the magazine and you'll see whether they are interested mainly in home-making or relationships. Are readers younger and socially mobile, or older and settled? What kind of holidays and jobs are featured? Is the editorial style factual or restrained, chatty or gushy?

For magazine short stories, don't just plunge in with any short story you have written. Study the magazines you are aiming at – *Take a Break* and *The Lady* have short story slots but, although their stories do have strands in common, the tone is different.

Essential ads

Advertisements, as we've seen, provide a vital window into a magazine's short story DNA. It's where you can work out, roughly, where the short story reader is in age, attitude and spending power.

Key trio

It's in the trio of letters, ads and content that you find the magazine's *attitude* – the all-important key to getting your writing accepted here. It's an attitude to all aspects of life – relationships, money, family life – that the magazine will display. By reviewing the three key aspects of the magazine – letters, advertisement and contents – you can get an excellent feel for the title . . . and for the short story it would carry.

Construct your story with a definite start, middle, end. Keep thinking 'what happens next?' Keep throwing problems at your main character. Even at the end, the reader should want to read on. Above all, magazine readers want a satisfying read. Stories could be set centuries ago, or in the future, or you could create a short story via a series of emails, or Tweets.

Angles and ideas editors say 'yes' to!

Three winning ways

1. Get some emotion into the first paragraph.

2. Surprises – magazine editors like them. Even if you're writing on a well-worn topic, strive for a new and surprising fact. I found out only recently that the first English coronation was held in Bath, not London – in 973AD, the coronation of King Edgar.

3. Anything that can be picked out and promoted on the cover – known as a coverline – will be even more tempting to the magazine editor you're trying to impress. Use 'number' pieces – 9 can't fail housework short cuts; 7 dilemmas to avoid at work; 5 easy steps to happiness; 5 stress-free weekends; 7 ways to live well on a student grant.

'Advertisements, as we've seen, provide a vital window into a magazine's short story DNA. It's where you can work out, roughly, where the short story reader is in age, attitude and spending power.'

'Anything that can be picked out and promoted on the cover – known as a coverline – will be even more tempting to the magazine editor you're trying to impress. Use 'number' pieces – 9 can't fail housework shortcuts; 7 dilemmas to avoid at work: 5 easy steps to happiness: 5 stress-free weekends; 7 ways to live well on student grant.'

Summing Up

▨ You can start your magazine career with a reader's letter – many writers have.

▨ 'Think' pieces are another good way to begin your magazine writing.

▨ Try short taster travel pieces as an entrée to travel writing.

▨ Plan some articles in terms of 'number' pieces which can be promoted on the magazine cover.

▨ Study magazines for reader profile, and aim short stories at this particular reader.

▨ Keep short stories moving by throwing problem after problem at your main character.

Chapter Four

Crafting Carefully

Clever crafting is vital. That means writing in magazine-ese, creating compelling intros, proofing your work . . . all tools of the trade that can be picked up like a language! Your greatest work aid here is constantly reading and re-reading the magazines you hope will accept your work. Study the article introductions, the endings, the length of paragraphs and the type of adjectives used. Don't ever stop reading magazines.

Grab your reader

Essentially, a magazine is an easy read. It's not an academic thesis or a novel. It's something to relax with, and pick up and put down easily. Here's a key principle to remember:

- Nothing that can't be absorbed at first reading ever appears in a magazine.

How to achieve this simple, easy-to-understand writing smoothness? When you begin your piece, first identify its emotional tone and keep checking that you're keeping to your own brief. Is the emotional tone witty, wistful, angry, triumphant, critical?

Emotion first

Structure your feature with a quote – first person always works. You can bring your own experience into play in anything from an article on hairdressing (how you once had a terrible cut at an expensive hair salon) to strategies for phobic flyers. In every case, begin at a point of action with emotion in your first sentence, and a reason for the reader to read on, like this:

'I've always been terrified of flying. I admit it. But here I am at 30,000 feet looking down on the Alps. And my palms aren't damp, nor am I waiting desperately for the drinks trolley or reaching for a pill.'

The final paragraph is important, too. Here you might reach a clear conclusion, pose a question or speculate about the future.

'Hypnotherapy worked on my flying phobia for that journey. But three flights later, I feel a small twinge of fear creeping back. Yes, I've booked for a therapy top-up! At £65 a session, it's not cheap. But is it worth it? Without a doubt.'

Key pointers

Here are the four staple craft pointers:

- A short sentence is an easy sentence.
- A whole idea is contained in each sentence or paragraph.
- Full stops and commas are the greatest aids to clarity and readability.
- Good magazine writing is vigorous writing.

As Strunk and White wrote in *The Elements of Style* (Macmillan, 1935) the as yet unrivalled American handbook on English usage:

'Vigorous writing is concise. A sentence should contain no unnecessary words, a paragraph no unnecessary sentences, for the same reason that a drawing should have no unnecessary lines and a machine no unnecessary parts'.

Grab your reader by writing emotion or tension into your first sentences.

'It's seven in the evening of a glorious hot day in Seville. I'm sitting nervously in the front row, waiting for my first bullfight to begin. My wife backed out at the last minute. Drums sound, and the sombre procession of toreadors into the ring unfolds . . .'

Break it up!

Decide how you'll break up the piece – with a whole idea in each paragraph. The idea-in-every-paragraph technique sounds crude, but it will help you to focus on getting the piece onto your screen. Write an outline of the paragraphs, and what will go in each.

Intros and endings

Writing the introduction to any piece is usually the hardest part. As always, the first step to starting to write is the steepest. You have an idea; you're at your desk, you know what you're going to write about, so how to begin your article?

I recommend writing out the 'running order' of your piece in longhand first. You may even like to do it in points, with a couple of sentences for each point. Writing out your running order first could make it much easier for you to follow when you do your final version.

So, each time you write an article, draft out a 'plot' – with that running order – first. Draw a rough plan of your article, outlining each complete idea – no matter how small – that will go into each paragraph. The plot is the 'story' of your article, with a beginning, middle and end.

Hello hierarchy

Introduce your ideas in a 'hierarchy' – with the most arresting or original fact or idea first, then the others in descending order of significance.

It's the way you'd tell a friend about something that's happened – with the most dramatic fact first, followed by the other bits of information in diminishing order of importance.

Neat writing tips

Knock one sentence into two for your opening paragraph. In most cases, the improvement will be 100%.

Your opening paragraph is crucial. It:

- Attracts your audience.
- Signals what your work will be about without being too detailed.
- Attempts to involve the audience.

This is an intro paragraph from *Take a Break* – a health story by Claire Hicklin. *Take a Break* pays £200 for each reader's story on health.

'I stared at the pregnancy test, willing the second blue line to appear. Nothing. I had been trying to get pregnant for almost ten years, and every month I was disappointed'.

'Structure your feature with a quote – first person always works. You can bring your own experience into play in anything from an article on hairdressing (how you once had a terrible cut at an expensive hair salon) to strategies for phobic flyers.'

This opening paragraph attracts the audience – how many millions of women will identify with this situation? It tells you what the topic is, and involves the reader from the start. It is crisp, honest, employs strong emotions and makes you want to read on. It goes straight away to the heart of the story.

When you have completed your piece write the one word – Ends – after the final paragraph. This tells the editor there's no more to come.

Simple subbing and proofing

Subbing is a revision and checking process that ensures the article is ready for publication. Magazines and newspapers used to employ large teams of sub-editors who would check your work – spelling, grammar, punctuation and facts – for you.

This safety net is being reduced and in some places even taken down, as publishers look to writers to handle the basic subbing and proofing themselves. There might be one multi-skilled sub-editor who can do a little work on your article, but the less there is for him or her to do, the better.

It all means extra work for the writer, but editors will favour freelance writers whose work requires minimum revision. Learn to do your own subbing thoroughly, and your prospects for getting your articles accepted will be much greater.

What are the aims of professional subbing? There are four main ones:

- To ensure that everything that can be checked has been checked – phone numbers, websites, dates, name spellings and statistics. Your article must be accurate.

- To ensure that there's nothing in the article that is a potential libel, or offensive.

- To clarify text that is unclear in its meaning.

- To make your feature fit the number of words required. Read articles in the magazine you aim at and count the number of words in the published features. Then make sure your feature is not longer or very much shorter. There's no point in sending a 10,000-word feature to a magazine that never runs anything longer than 2,500. In many cases, on weekly women's magazines, articles won't be more than 750-1,000 words.

Superb proofing

Subbing on screen can be done speedily, and you can use the time-saving word count. But do not rely on your computer's spelling and punctuation checkers. These can be an unreliable guide through the minefields of the English – and American! – language. So write and first sub your article on screen, print it, read it again on paper, mark the corrections on the paper version, and then amend on screen. You will be looking out for:

- Spelling mistakes.
- Adjectives, nouns and verbs that you have repeated in the same sentence or paragraph.
- Punctuation errors.
- Words or phrases that are unlikely to be understood by readers.
- Over-long sentences.
- Mixed-up tenses.
- Verb confusion.

Do not expect to sub your article to perfection in one go – I will do three or four subbings before I'm convinced an article is as perfect as I can get it. With each subbing, you hone and crisp up your article.

Copy checklist

Here's a checklist to complete before you hit send:

1. Check telephone numbers and website addresses you've included. Do not assume they're right because they were in a leaflet.

2. Ask people you interview to spell out his or her name. Even a simple name that sounds like Carol, Lisa or Jacky can be spelt in several ways. Is it Jill or Gill? Clare or Claire? Lisa or Liza? Sarah or Sara? The worst thing is to have Lisa and Liza when you are writing about the same person.

3. Look up street spellings on a local map or local directory.

4. Carefully check prices of everything you mention, whether it's a cheap meal deal, the price of a budget flight to Spain or a supermarket sandwich. It may not seem that crucial to you – but the people involved can get upset if details go in wrongly . . . and so can readers.

5. Information on a website can be useful sometimes, but it will not compare with talking to an expert. Website information can be inaccurate, and also goes out of date quickly.

Boxes and bars

Women's magazines love tip boxes and sidebars . . . they make the page look good. Tip boxes, sidebars and fact boxes might summarise aspects of the main feature, or carry additional information.

You can also do your sidebars as 'dos and don'ts', or as 'Yes to' . . . and 'No to' . . . lists.

Picture this!

If you are taking photos you intend to send to magazines – especially magazines printed on glossy paper – you'll need more than just any old digital camera. Magazines can use only high resolution images – a minimum of 300 dpi (that's dots per inch). If the resolution is lower than that, the picture quality will deteriorate when it's used at the large size the editor might want – and which the picture might merit.

You can make the picture look as big as you want on your computer screen, but that doesn't mean it's a high resolution shot.

Sorry, but pictures taken on mobile phones and from websites (even if you do own the copyright) will not be good enough.

Summing Up

- Grab your reader with the first sentences – inject emotion.

- Every story and feature needs a beginning, middle and end.

- Introduce your article ideas in a 'hierarchy' – with the most dramatic fact first.

- Add sidebars, dos and don'ts, fact boxes to your magazine articles – editors love them.

- Images for magazines must be a minimum of 300 dpi.

- Check, check and check again for accuracy of facts you use.

'Subbing on screen can be done speedily, and you can use the time-saving word count. But do not rely on your computer's spelling and punctuation checkers. These can be an unreliable guide through the minefields of the English – and American! – language.'

Chapter Five

Be the Favourite Freelancer!

How much would your self-confidence be improved if you knew you were an editor's favourite freelancer? Think that's impossible? Don't – you already have all the skills!

Freelance writing is an area in which emotions and the way you convey your personality can play a crucial part.

I have sabotaged at least two promising professional relationships in the past by answering the phone in a short-tempered way, and being dismissive of a feature editor's queries about my work. This resulted in me losing a column I had valued – what a huge mistake I made. It was a long time ago, but I learned from it. The trouble is, once you've had 'words' things are never the same again. Try not to have them!

Now I make sure, when I'm in my freelance role, that no matter how simple, apparently trivial or inconvenient the query from an editor might be, my answer is always a polite yes. And when I'm in editor mode, I try to be courteous, helpful and generous with advice with writers.

The importance of being likeable and being liked is vital in freelance journalism. Being patient, tolerant, polite . . . they are all crucial virtues. Freelancers can win or lose work by the way they deal with an editor.

The first thing to learn about being the favourite freelancer is that it doesn't involve being pushy. When I started in journalism, the popular theory was that the harder you pushed, the more likely you were to succeed in the glamorous world of media. Not true. Yes, you need self-confidence – it's not the right profession for you if you are very shy – but strangers warm to you only if you

'Women's magazines love tip boxes and sidebars . . . they make the page look good.'

are not overpowering. When we meet someone new, we're more likely to talk to him or her if they're non-threatening, not overbearing and have a pleasant voice and smile.

Being modest and quiet opens doors for us, while being forceful and pushy can get them slammed in our face. The best description I've heard of the favourite freelancer (from an editor of *The Lady*) was this: 'Tried, tested and trusted'.

What does it all boil down to? Good manners – it's that simple.

Here are my three cardinal rules:

1. Don't be pushy . . . It's not being pushy that makes you popular with editors – it's being polite. Perfect manners will take you a long way – and keep you there.

2. Make your first approach by letter or email, not by telephone. Attach your CV, a selection (no more than four) of any cuttings you may have, and three feature ideas for the magazine. If you don't hear back within a month, follow it with a polite email.

3. Don't pester. It's tempting to try to find out what they're doing with your piece! Magazines can seem arrogant or disorganised, or just uncaring. When you receive no verdict on your article or short story you feel frustrated and even angry. But don't give in to negative feelings. Or rather, give in and seethe in private, but never indulge the urge to send an angry email or make a cross phone call. Polite emails will elicit responses; angry phone calls will sabotage your relationship with the magazine. The best advice is to continue writing and submitting so that you always have several irons in the fire and aren't just hanging on for the verdict on one piece of work.

Follow all my tips, and you too can be the favourite freelancer! Begin by pitching well. You've prepared your ideas, now you need to send them to a magazine by post or email with a covering letter. The cover letter is important. It should be as clear and brief as possible. It's your pitch to the magazine.

When editors see a good cover letter, they know the work attached is likely to be good as well. A badly written cover letter is rarely followed by a usable feature.

Essential dos and don'ts

The ideal cover letter/pitch . . .

- Is pleasant, not pushy.
- Outlines the content precisely and briefly.
- Doesn't grill the editor for dates when the piece might be used.
- Does not ask for anything to be returned (if you are submitting by post, make sure you send only copies, not originals).
- Does not assume that the piece will be snapped up instantly – it's good to be a little modest.
- Is short and succinct!

Practical pitch

This pitch could be made to a weekly women's magazine, a pets' magazine, or popular newspaper supplement. The modern pitch is combined with the cover letter, to make it speedy for editors to read. Overleaf is an example.

'Don't pester. It's tempting to try to find out what they're doing with your piece! Magazines can seem arrogant or disorganised, or just uncaring. When you receive no verdict on your article or short story you feel frustrated and even angry. Don't give in to negative feelings. Or rather, give in and seethe in private, but never indulge the urge to send an angry email or make a cross phone call.'

> Dear Editor (find out the correct name by checking with the magazine – one of the cardinal sins is writing to an editor who's no longer there, or spelling his or her name incorrectly)
>
> Past Perfect Pets – pitch
>
> I'm in the graveyard of a Wiltshire church, wandering round a pets' graveyard. There are tributes to much-loved kittens and dogs of centuries ago, and even to owls and robins.
>
> Their memorials range from sentimental to witty, and I've been able to research background material on some of the 'celebrity' pets and their owners. Would a piece on this work for you?
>
> I have been published in my local county magazine and in *Yours* magazine – some cuttings are attached. In 2001, I won first prize in a writing competition run by a national writers' magazine: my background is in primary school teaching.
>
> I can supply by email high-resolution images of most of the pets' tombstones, and have also researched some images of several of the high-profile owners. A short CV and a picture of me are also included, just in case it's of use to you.
>
> Kind regards . . .

Don't forget to include your name, address and phone numbers . . . even in email. This letter is a good template because:

- It opens with a short window into the topic, grabbing the editor's attention and written in the style of the magazine.

- There's an explanation of the research for the feature in the second paragraph. Mini case studies of some celebrity pets and owners are included.

- There are details of the writer's previously published work, and of an award she has won. Never be shy about mentioning any previous work or prizes – it's a great help to an editor.

- The writer offers information about her own job. If you are not working, you could mention an interest or hobby. This is always useful to know: it's a window into you, and your usefulness to the magazine.

- The letter explains that the writer can supply high resolution images – vital for a feature like this.

- She includes a brief CV and a picture of herself. Many magazines use picture by-lines – readers love to see who has written what they are reading – and if you need it in first, that's another job the editor doesn't have to worry about.

- The entire pitch is summed up in just 152 words.

Market with success

Beginner writers are often worried about sending out ideas, thinking that the magazine will 'steal' them. I have never known this happen – most editors are only too eager for good ideas written well. But you need to recognise that often several people will have the same idea at the same time.

When there's a national event – like a royal wedding or the Olympic Games – it's to be expected that several magazine and newspaper writers and editors will get similar ideas at the same time. If you see 'your' idea published under someone else's name and with their research, it won't be theft, only a case of great minds thinking alike. The trick is to get your ideas in first. Think well ahead for seasonal ideas and commemorative ideas. As soon as you have a brilliant idea, get the pitch ready.

Excellent email

When you write to a magazine by email, it must be impeccable. In general, using email has led to a marked deterioration of grammar and use of English. We hurl off emails with obvious spelling mistakes and don't bother to correct them – we'd never do that in a letter.

But editors notice errors, and they will assume you are sloppy and lack attention to detail.

'When editors see a good cover letter/ pitch, they know the work attached is likely to be good as well. A badly written cover letter/pitch is rarely followed by a usable feature.'

Market you!

Here's an often-ignored first step in providing what magazine editors want to know. Every time you submit your work on spec to a magazine – from a reader's letter to full-length feature or a short story – always include a brief CV, or little 'press release', and a warm photo of you as a JPEG or a print. It could be just a simple portrait (always smiling) or a more posed full-length shot.

Try to tailor your picture to your topics – if you write about your kids, get a picture with them. If it's food, you need an apron and saucepan. Writing about working from home? Get your laptop into the photo. Don't be shy about this – smiling pictures of you – and your child if relevant – will improve your chances of getting published in a women's magazine.

Once you've got your pictures and have worked out your brief marketing letter, store it safely on your computer – and perhaps keep a copy on a disc or flash drive. It's there ready to send out every time you submit a piece. Your letter can be adjusted to suit the magazine you're sending your work to.

Key phrases

Key phrases could be 'fanatical cleaner', 'mother of four', 'cookery competition winner', 'salsa fan', 'coach travel expert', 'Open University addict' – anything that indicates your areas of interest and expertise. Anything that an editor could hook to a feature. Anything that might be a possible cover line.

Here's how:

Linda Mason, (include address, email, phone – add these to every communication).

Linda Mason of Bristol asked for an unusual wedding anniversary gift for her 20th wedding anniversary – a course in bee-keeping. A keen gardener who also runs an allotment, she teaches French to adults. Last year she won a short story competition for her local writers' circle. She is married with a daughter of 18.

That's all you need! This, plus your picture and a cover note on your article adds 100% more to your submission. Editors love these sorts of writers . . . writers who show some understanding of the way magazines operate. If you also have a website and a blog, this is a definite marketing extra – editors, agents and publishers do look at blogs.

Be businesslike

Yes, it's a creative industry – but you'll make friends and influence editors by being businesslike. That means pictures supplied as transparencies or prints being sent by Special Delivery – normal postal deliveries can't be relied on these days – and with accurate, informative captions. If you're sending them on a disc or by email, include a file with a list identifying each picture.

Always find a way to identify pictures – if prints, a sticky label; if digitals, with a number that relates to a caption. Put each transparency in a separate envelope.

Editors hate being told on the phone by someone to whom they have given a commission that the feature can't be done – three days from deadline! Always be reliable.

If you have a website, can you put the magazines you write for on it? Offer them a link? Think in terms of making partnerships with the editors you write for, rather than building up a 'them and me' scenario.

Practical checklist

- Put all of your contact details on every communication you send, from a one-line email to a feature. That's name, address, phone number and email address.

- Once you have filed your article, try not to keep sending amendments and revisions – don't even send one unless it's essential. To avoid this, just do two things – read the copy twice at an hour's interval, checking all the facts.

- If you can leave it overnight, read it again the next day. Then send it.

- Always ring or email them back very promptly if they leave a message for you to do so – don't leave it until the next day.

- Keep copy deadlines pinned up on your noticeboard. If you have a regular column, keep working well ahead. If you can get a whole issue ahead, you'll certainly be one of the editor's favourites.

Good to talk

You've sent off your cover letter and the editor, or a member of staff, phones to talk to you. Or you need to phone the magazine. Panic! Many freelance writers dread speaking to editors on the phone. Even if you get through, it's easy to be overwhelmed with nerves.

Here are three simple ways to sail through the phone call:

- Slow down when you speak, and don't start laughing when you realise who it is – nerves can sometimes do that to us.
- Keep your voice low if you know you have a tendency to be high pitched or shrill when nervous.
- Try not to mention the weather, holidays or anything not germane to the call – unless the editor does, of course.

'Every time you submit your work on spec to a magazine – from a reader's letter to full-length feature or a short story – always include a brief CV or little 'press release' and a warm photo of you, as a JPEG or a print. It could be just a simple portrait (always smiling) or a more posed full-length shot.'

Summing Up

- Your marketing starts with the clever cover letter.

- Send a picture of you with every submission, and an engaging few lines about you – your 'press release'.

- Don't worry too much about your ideas being 'stolen' – and accept that sometimes rivals writers will have the same idea.

- Strive to be the favourite freelancer – pleasant, not pushy!

'Once you have filed your article, try not to keep sending amendments and revisions – don't even send one unless it's essential. To avoid this, just do two things – read the copy twice at an hour's interval, checking all the facts.'

Chapter Six

Manage Your Time

How much time do you have to write?

Ever heard anyone say, 'I'd love to write for magazines, but I just don't have time'. If you have whole days, weekends, one day a week or even less – then you've got time to write! But however much or little time you have, it's vital to use it with discipline . . . frittering it away is easy to do.

The trick is to treat your writing as a professional job. How much would you be paid at work if you simply sat and stared your computer, or kept on popping out to the shops? Look on your writing time as a finite resource.

Make a routine

Decide now how much time you can spend on writing – one day a week, every morning, three evenings or an hour a day? Pick achievable systems. If you know you're hopeless at getting up early, don't plan on being an early-bird writer. But if you like to stay up late reading, you could convert this into writing, and do a couple of late nights a week.

If you are home-based, it's best not to give all of your waking hours over to writing; you might become jaded. Instead, decide to write, let's say, for three days a week from 10 to 4, and do chores and contrasting activities for the remaining time. As your writing develops and you have success, your patterns may change – but start with a routine that is manageable and not oppressive.

Make the most of the time you have

Type a time table

A written timetable is essential. Put it on your pinboard, or keep it in your diary. Your writer's timetable is like making appointments with yourself – you must show up! As Woody Allen said, 80% of success is showing up. If you fritter away your writing time and don't keep to a time table, it doesn't matter how talented you are – you'll never see the words on paper, which means editors won't, either.

Simple space

You've decided when you'll write and written down that timetable for yourself – in your diary. You need a 'sacred' space during the evenings or at weekends when you write up your experiences and plot your article or short story. Those pages need to grow each week – that's the main thing. Keep a brief record of what you write.

Stick to an achievable goal, completing an article per week or month. Make initial notes and any extra research the first day, then develop your structure, write the piece, and polish and submit it on the final day.

At the end of each writing session, make a note in your diary of just what you did – so that you can see your work mounting up, and you'll know you are keeping to your plan.

Streamline your other chores.

Time-wasters for the writer

Many new writers find that starting to write is their biggest problem. Displacement activities – little chores, making cups of coffee, checking Facebook – suddenly seem enticing. If it's a sunny day, you can become restless just sitting at your desk. You suddenly feel the urgent need to stock up the fridge.

Don't worry – it's the same for all writers. The good news is that once you begin to write, energy starts to seep through you and you lose yourself in your writing.

Warning – these are the top time-wasters:

- Constantly logging on to your email.
- Checking Yahoo news.
- Logging on to Facebook.
- Answering the phone – keep it switched off, and sign up with the Telephone Preference Service to stop sales calls.
- Getting up to do housework.
- Making too many coffees or teas – stick to one per session.
- Computer games.
- Starting too late – use an alarm clock to get up early.
- Going out for snacks and sweets – keep a supply in-house!

Max your writing time

Working and writing?

So you're working, maybe in a 9 to 5 or part-time job, or studying . . . and you're writing, too. It could be short stories, articles, or trying out readers' letters or points of view pieces.

But sometimes the energy just isn't there – you'll sit and stare at the computer, flick through your notebook or gaze out of the window. You might even be sidetracked by non-essential tasks – start to paint a window sill, turn out a cupboard, or just feel like having a nap! Because you have your paid job as well, it's easy to feel that time outside of that really ought to be time when you should be relaxing. Your writing may even begin to feel like an extra chore.

Use your job to help your writing – keep that little notebook with you at all times!

Dialogue, dialogue, dialogue – jot down snatches of conversation you hear on buses or trains, in the queue at the bank, office-speak, arguments, flirtations, complaints. You'll often hear expressions and exchanges that inspire your writer's imagination. Again, you might think you will remember, but unless you write it down, you'll probably forget.

Build up your words

If you keep putting words on your screen, you build up and create articles and stories. If you keep thinking about it, but never take action, you don't! It's as simple as that – in theory. In practice, it takes lots of discipline, but the good news is that the more you do it, the more enjoyable you'll find it becomes.

'A written timetable is essential. Put it on your pinboard, or keep it in your diary.'

Top tips

- Writing when you have a paid job is all about discipline. It's a question of setting a time-table and sticking to it. There will be bad days, but you will recover. It's important not to give up.

- Physical exercise is also vital – you don't want to fall into the trap of just doing your day job, and writing. Add some walking, cycling or swimming at least three times a week. Another brain-refresher is painting or drawing – since it uses a different part of your mind.

One-day-a-week writer

One day a week to write – luxury! Look on this day as a pleasure – but plan ahead and prepare for it. You need it to write – so get the household chores and shopping done the day before. That means you can wake up and go straight to your desk knowing everything is in place. You can begin.

If, at weekends, you can permit yourself an entire day without interruptions (you should have your food in, and basic chores completed) you will find you work at least 30% better . . . that's according to Patricia Highsmith, author of *Plotting and Writing Suspense Fiction*. Switch the phone off, don't open up emails, forget the Internet, and don't respond to the doorbell!

This weekend schedule could become a habit – one you will begin to enjoy . . . perhaps not at first, but as the discipline increases, so does the pleasure.

Ten-minute writer

It is possible to keep on writing even through a deluge of extra work at the office, and it's important to do so – keep flexing those writing muscles and writing becomes a habit, a pleasure. But if you let that habit go even for a few days, it's so much harder to re-start the engine.

It's best if your 10 minutes is at the same time every day – say first thing in the morning or last thing at night – but that's not essential. According to scientific research, it takes 21 days to form a new habit – so don't expect it to be easy instantly! If you can go on for longer than 10 minutes, that's fine. Don't feel you must stop after the prescribed time.

Let's say that in 10 minutes you manage 100 words. That doesn't sound a lot, but in a five-day week, it's 500, and in three weeks, 1,500 words – more than enough, edited down, for an average magazine or newspaper article of between 750 and 1,200 words.

Summing Up

'Keep that little notebook with you at all times! Dialogue, dialogue, dialogue – jot down snatches of conversation you hear on buses or trains, in the queue at the bank, office-speak, arguments, flirtations, complaints. You'll often hear expressions and exchanges that inspire your writer's imagination.'

- Decide how much time you have to write – two days a week, one day, less?
- Make a time-table for your writing.
- Show up at your computer at the allotted time.
- Outlaw the time-wasters.
- Keep your writer's notebook with you 24/7.

Chapter Seven

Legal and Admin Matters

Legal matters (libel, copyright, privacy) and admin (keeping records, building up a library) are important to the magazine writer. My admin isn't the most streamlined in the world, I admit it! But it can take half an hour a day just to find notes and references for an article you're working on if you don't keep things reasonably straight. That's what I've learned to my cost!

New writers often worry about libel and copyright laws, but you shouldn't be overanxious about these. As you're writing magazine features and short stories – and not breaking news – you are unlikely to run into trouble on either front, but it's good to be aware of the basic rules.

A look at the law

Libel law (Defamation)

Can be and often is very complicated and ruinously expensive for everyone involved – writers, publishers and plaintiffs – even before a case gets to court. In brief, a libel is the publication of a statement which even by implication wrongly damages someone's reputation and livelihood.

The laws of libel in England have evolved over the centuries, but their fundamental purpose has remained unchanged since Shakespeare's time. He writes, in Othello:

'Good name in man and woman, dear my lord, is the immediate jewel of their souls. Who steals my purse steals trash; 'tis something, nothing; 'Twas mine, 'tis his, and has been slave to thousands. But he that filches from me my good name robs me of that which not enriches him and makes me poor indeed'.

'Writing when you have a paid job is all about discipline. It's a question of setting a time-table and sticking to it. There will be bad days, but you will recover. It's important not to give up.'

There are a handful of legal defences to libel claims, the best of which is that what has been published – in print or online – is true. But believing or even knowing it is true is not sufficient: the writer and publisher must be able to prove it is true. Doing so can often be costly . . . and sometimes impossible.

Fair comment based on fact is another defence but – again – the crucial word is fact. A fair comment based on supposition, rumour or speculation defence will not stand up in court.

Copyright law

Exists to protect the ownership rights of people who have created written, theatrical, musical and artistic works. It also covers photographs, films, book layouts, sound recordings and broadcasts, and it applies to creative work published on the Internet.

As a writer, you might want to use a quotation or a passage from a book or play by another published author. You can do this without getting permission from the copyright owner, provided the passage is not excessively long – keep it to no more than three or four paragraphs – and the original work and author is acknowledged. Photographs cannot be used without the permission of the copyright owner.

At the time of going to press, the conflict in English law between privacy and freedom of expression remains unresolved. Litigation in the civil courts in both of these areas is made possible by the European Convention of Human Rights (ECHR), which is currently part of English and Scottish law. Article 8 states that 'everyone has the right to respect for private and family life', while Article 10 upholds the right to freedom of expression.

Calls for a home-made English privacy law have to date gone unanswered. Judges, meanwhile, are tending to interpret ECHR law as a ban on publishing material that invades personal privacy unless it can be justified as a matter of genuine public interest – and that does not mean merely something in which the public is interested, such as the lurid details of the sex lives of film stars or footballers.

As a freelance writer, the copyright of the articles and stories you write and sell is yours . . . unless you sign it away to a publisher.

Do that admin!

When it's left to get out of control, paperwork can clobber you and keep
you from your main interest – writing. Searching for stuff can be tiring and
dispiriting as well as time-consuming. Here are some tips on making sure
admin doesn't stop you doing what you really want to be doing.

Keep records.

Maintain a simple record list of the pieces you send out (whether
commissioned or sent on spec), with dates, publications – plus the results:
acceptances, rejections, acknowledgements – and keep it all updated. You'll
need to send invoices for articles you have had accepted.

The simplest invoices are best – just a sheet of A4 paper headed with your
name, address, phone number and email address, followed by the title of the
piece, the fee (if you know what that will be). Add a line saying when the article
was commissioned and by whom. Number and date your invoice. Invoices
do sometimes go astray in publishing houses, so a separate number for each
invoice is important.

Keeping a picture library on your computer? Ensure you always have the
latest version. Make folders for each magazine. Keep a record of what was
used in which magazine. Keep a record of your articles' sources, too; those
contacts could always come in handy again. Send photocopies of the articles
to the people you have written about, and to those who supplied valuable
information. They'll be happy to help you again.

Keep a file of editors' names, addresses, phone numbers and email addresses
– and keep it updated. Articles and stories sent to an editor who emigrated to
New Zealand ten years ago will start you off on a bad note . . . it looks as though

'New writers
often worry
about libel
and copyright
laws, but you
shouldn't be
overanxious
about these. As
you're writing
magazine
features and
short stories –
and not breaking
news – you are
unlikely to run
into trouble on
either front, but
it's good to be
aware of the
basic rules.'

you don't read the magazine. If an editor's name doesn't clearly indicate his or her gender, find out before you write to them. Is that Sam for Samuel or Samantha? Is it Mr or Ms? Most magazines have photos of their editors on the 'welcome' page.

Set up a separate list of accounts department details and how they pay you – BACS or cheques? Magazine groups do change hands – and accounts departments can change too.

If the idea of paperwork, records and invoices worries you, join the club – its membership is massive! Most writers love writing, but hate admin. The trick is to have a simple and logical storage system. If computer folders and files get out of hand, keep a ring-bound folder with paper copies of invoices. Some writers prefer this instant access to their records.

De-junk that desk!

Once you have correspondence, source material and invoices, your desk can easily resemble a dustbin. This is an instant de-junk plan:

- Clear the top first – it's not a storage area! Just leave your computer, notebook and notes, and pens. This will instantly make you feel more efficient.

- Keep ongoing matters – tax etc – in a ring-bound folder. Use these folders for most things, and store them all together, upright. You can buy them in bright colours for around 99p in supermarkets. This is such a good way to store – rather than tottering piles of jumbled papers.

- Re-locate machines or gadgets you don't absolutely need on your desk – keep that desk top as uncluttered as possible.

> ### Top tip
>
> Need a new desk? Brown furniture can have a slightly depressing effect, especially if it's a desk you have had for a long time. A glass-topped trestle table is an ideal choice for writing – everything seems so much lighter! You may even be able to find one in a junk or second-hand shop.

'There are a handful of legal defences to libel claims, the best of which is that what has been published – in print or online – is true. But believing or even knowing it is true is not sufficient: the writer and publisher must be able to prove it is true. Doing so can often be costly . . . and sometimes impossible.'

Legal to recycle?

A frequent question is, 'Can I sell an article more than once? Is it legal to do this?'

Yes, it is called recycling, something that seems to make many freelance or hobby writers nervous. There's no need to be. Most articles can be re-worked with a new angle, thus increasing your revenue and your profile.

What you may need to do is look further afield for your second and subsequent markets – they could be trade magazines, professional newsletters, travel magazines, niche family magazines, hobby magazines or newspapers.

These are called secondary markets. The first sale of a feature about having a grandchild to stay for the first time could be to a mainstream magazine such as *Woman's Weekly*. A secondary sale could be to *Saga*, the magazine specifically for older readers, many of whom will be grandparents.

A third might be a magazine only for grandparents, while a fourth could be a local magazine for retired people (in which case you would pick local places to visit, or local cafés and restaurants suitable for the grandparent/grandchild duo). There's more on techniques for this in chapter 10.

Write your main feature for the market that pays best and/or has the biggest profile and largest circulation – they're not always the same – then re-work it for other likely markets. Add fresh quotes to freshen up the piece.

'Keeping a picture library on your computer? Ensure you always have the latest version. Make folders for each magazine. Keep a record of what was used in which magazine. Keep a record of your articles' sources, too; those contacts could always come in handy again.'

'If the idea of paperwork, records and invoices worries you, join the club – its membership is massive! Most writers love writing, but hate admin. The trick is to have a simple and logical storage system. If computer folders and files get out of hand, keep a ring-bound folder with paper copies of invoices. Some writers prefer this instant access to their records.'

Summing Up

■ Re-locate machines or gadgets you don't absolutely need on your desk – keep that desk as uncluttered as possible.

■ You are legally free to recycle your articles – you own the copyright – as long as you change the wording and rejig them. Use the content again but change the structure. It's best to add a fresh quote or two.

■ Write your main feature for the market that pays best and/or has the biggest profile and largest circulation, then re-work it for other likely markets.

■ Send photocopies of your articles to people you've written about – they'll be happy to help you again.

Chapter Eight

Welcome to the eMag!

There are thousands of eMagazines – from *Call Centre Helper* (a lively magazine for call centre workers) to the WeightWatchers magazine for, well, weight watchers! Just like the print ones, they all need copy.

It can be easier to get published on the Web, since the overheads in online publication are vastly lower than their print equivalents. They do not need huge investments in presses, paper, ink and delivery trucks, but their circulation is global. They can put in new features every day if they want to, instead of every fortnight or month. At the same time, they pay a lot less and many don't pay at all. Publication does give you profile, help you build up readership.

A print magazine has a finite number of pages. Their online editions are not restricted in this way. If you've got a special subject, they may not be able to make room for a column in the main magazine, but could in the online one.

If you want to write for the Web, it's a good idea to have your own blog. It's a quick way for a magazine editor to assess your writing style. In the past, editors looked at writers' paper cuttings – increasingly they view their blogs.

Internet writing style

Writing for the Web has evolved a set of requirements different from print publishing. Writing for the Web magazine is economic and spare . . . vigorous.

You need fewer words. Less is more. Take what you would write for print, and cut it in half. Then cut it in half again! It sounds drastic, but the researchers who study people's Web reading habits insist on this formula.

It's essential that readers want to navigate to your article. Unlike a print magazine, the eMag doesn't stay on the sofa ready for you to pick up and put down. Either readers read an entire Web article at once – or they don't read it at all. Readers with smartphones are reading on the go and want quick compelling information – so it's vital that they don't lose interest.

Blog matters

'Send photocopies of your articles to the people you have written about, and to those who supplied valuable information. They'll be happy to help you again.'

Blogs are becoming a greater asset for a magazine writer. A writer with a blog has a readily available folder of ideas for an editor to look at instantly. But you need to pour your life into the blog!

It helps if you have a theme, for example travel, your family, a hobby. Then the more honesty, detail and freshness you can put in, the better. A blog should not read like an essay or a guidebook.

The discipline of writing every day or every week can't not help you as a magazine writer. And plenty of blogs have been turned into books – for example the blog by Belle du Jour – her blog became a magazine column and then a TV series starring Billie Piper.

Magazine editors look at blogs to identify new writing talent. But there are millions of blogs out there – so how do you get yours noticed by a magazine?

Ten tips for success:

1. Write with the reader in mind. Know about WIIFM? It's marketing jargon for What's In It For Me? That's what you should be keeping in mind. Your reader will read your post looking for what's in it for them.

2. Use words that everyone can understand. Avoid, replace, or define industry terms or other 'in-house' terminology. This includes acronyms. If the reader doesn't understand your words, they will tune you out.

3. People scan rather than read when reading online; their attention span is much shorter than when they read printed copy. Imagine people driving through your website at 60mph, treating the site as a series of billboards rather than reading it carefully.

4. Less is more. Remember – cut in half, then half again, what you'd write for a print journal.

5. Proofread for typos and glaring grammatical errors. It may mean you have to print out your material – it can be harder to spot mistakes on screen than on paper.

6. Keep it short and simple (KISS). You may have a lot to say and think it interesting, and it might be. But people are reading online and out of time. Get to the point quickly.

7. Keep it lively, make it snappy and snazzy. Keep in mind the journalist's rule of 5 Ws in the first paragraph or two: who, what, why, when and where.

8. Write clearly (short sentences, only one concept per sentence). No double speak or jargon; no more than one idea in one sentence– don't make your readers have to think about your meaning. Spoon-feed them. Use commas and dashes liberally.

9. Write as you talk. It's OK to use common expressions . . . but not obscene ones!

10. Polish every post. Is your blog as sparkling as it can be? Before you hit send, see if you can make it gleam even more.

Think first

Think hard about what you will blog about.

If you want to establish yourself as an expert in a field or topic area, then a more focused blog will be most suitable. But maybe you want to write about your life – as a student, a mother, an office worker. Fellow students, mothers, office workers will be your readership.

Check out other people's blogs on similar subjects – how will yours be different? Craft as carefully as you would for a magazine article. You can make your own life into a short story!

'Your own blog is a quick way for a magazine editor to assess your writing style. In the past editors looked at writers' paper cuttings – increasingly they view their blogs.'

You need to do three things for success:

- Write in the Internet style.
- Make each blog a satisfying read.
- Do all you can to grow a readership.

Internet proofing

Use this checklist to ask yourself questions as you are reading through your blog for typos and grammar:

- Will the topic be clear to someone who reads only the headline?
- Does the first paragraph indicate why the reader should care about it?
- Would someone who knows absolutely nothing about this topic understand this post?
- Is the post jargon-free?
- Have you peppered the headline and the post with keywords and phrases that will be attractive to search engines?
- Did you remember to ask your readers a question at the end, or something to stimulate readers to comment?
- Have you checked for repetition, spelling mistakes, errors?
- Did you remember to write with the reader in mind, always thinking WIIFT? (What's In It for Them?)

Grow your audience

Repeat visitors are very important in establishing your blog. Fly-by traffic is worthwhile, but building a loyal readership base is crucial. Make friends with other bloggers! Link to them and put comments on their sites.

Make the title engaging to the reader. More than anything else, the title determines whether or not people will click through from the search engines. Make it original. Online, it's the title that draws them in.

Network!

Socialise and network with others. Link often. This builds credibility and positions you as an expert in your field. People don't have time to know what others are doing, you should tell them. Linking to other blogs and websites also helps you build a network of associates who will in turn link to your blog.

Add pictures to your blog – pictures of you, pictures from your life, pictures which illustrate what you're blogging about. Think of each blog as a separate magazine article, with lively illustrations.

Join Twitter and Facebook and start a conversation with your readers. Make sure to reply to comments on your blog. By talking with your readers, you'll keep them checking back in and you'll be at the forefront of their minds, making them more likely to become a repeat visitor. Readers seeking out your words are invaluable for your career as a magazine writer.

eNumbers, and more . . .

Some basic Internet style points . . .

Numerals

Numerals (2, 3, etc.) are more likely to be read than numbers that are written out (two, three, etc.)

Lists

Use bullets or numbered lists: they are easy to scan. People notice the items at the top and the bottom the most.

Adjectives

Use them sparingly.

Editing

If you do the editing work, the reader won't have to. If you don't, the reader may not do the work (of reading) at all!

Avoid even a split second of confusion. 'Never ever leave the reader guessing' is advice I was given in my first week as a junior reporter on the Clevedon Mercury. It was the best advice then and it is now, whether you are writing for Web or for print publication.

Summing Up

- There's potential in eMagazines, and unlimited space for contributors.
- Print magazines which have a website presence are worth pitching to.
- Less is more – readers scan screens, so cut in half the word lengths you'd do for a print magazine.
- Grow your following by blogging and joining Twitter and Facebook.
- Ask readers questions to start a dialogue.
- Make your blog like a magazine article – but more economic.
- Proof your Internet work carefully.

'Make the title engaging to the reader. More than anything else, the title determines whether or not people will click through from the search engines. Make it original.'

'Use bullets or numbered lists: they are easy to scan. People notice the items at the top and the bottom the most.'

Chapter Nine

Coping with Rejection

Rejections hurt . . . but never let them defeat you.

An email from a publishing company lands in your in-box. Or a letter is on the doormat. What will it say? Can you bear to open it? Could it be a note telling you your work has been accepted . . . they actually want to publish you . . . you've won a writing competition? Fantastic!

But no, it's the dismal starkness of a rejection.

This is terrible news! The day darkens and your spirits plummet.

Is it worth bothering anymore? Is it worth going on? The piece you sent them was one of the best you'd ever written; it was exactly their tone and an original topic. So why on earth was it not accepted?

Don't hang on to pain

This pain can last all day, and longer. That's if you let it.

How productive will that be for you? Rejection is the biggest demon a writer must face. It's part of the writing package. I've had more rejections than I can bear to think about – including a rejection from a leading glossy magazine after I'd been told my article was accepted!

I've had unpleasant emails from editors, rude comments on my writing and confusing on-off signals from magazines. All upsetting at the time – until I remember that I've also had great compliments, follow-up commissions and regular column slots offered.

I've been 'the favourite freelance' at several magazines while getting a curt 'thanks but no thanks' from others. If you can't combat the inevitable downturn in spirits when you get the thumbs-down, you can't move on. The ability to deal with rejection is essential.

You are being your own worst enemy if you allow rejection to crush your writing endeavours. We all are that, from time to time. What helps is having practical strategies in place before you have to face rejection. You'll have these tactics as insurance. Think of it as making an investment in them now, so you can draw on them when they are needed.

Practical pointers

Quick-start tools

Feeling rejected this very minute?

Four things to make you feel better post-rejection right now:

1. Decide on one good thing to do today – it could be buying a stack of stationery, going to your favourite café for a caramel latte, making a last-minute date for lunch with a friend.

2. Draw through your doubts. Keep a sketchpad and art pencils handy. Do a rapid sketch – a cartoon or even just a face, which expresses how you are feeling. You can even do a nasty 'face' to represent the publication which rejected your article! Drawing uses a different part of your mind. It's calming and satisfying. Give it a try.

3. Buy a new novel, a how-to book, an author's biography – maybe from a market or charity bookstore.

4. Visit a free art gallery or museum and pick up some postcards which could inspire your writing.

It's good not to talk!

One of the headaches with rejection is that we often want to tell the world about it. We go on about it to family, mull over it and moan to friends. And what you focus on, you get more of. If rejection distresses you totally, you'll always be spiralling down into depression.

So, what's it to be? Wallow in rejection, or move on?

Don't do it!

If you want to improve your mood, don't:

- Phone a friend – Two of you focusing on the rejection may magnify it even more.

- Email a friend – Unless the answer is exactly what you want, this could do more harm than good. Email is so imperfect when emotions are involved. Your email of misery may get one back along the lines of 'pull yourself together', 'I had one worse than that' – or you never even get a reply, which is likely to be even worse.

- Contact the journal which rejected your work – If you want a guaranteed way to get on their 'trouble' list, this is it. Often, there's just no answer to 'What did I do wrong?' Even if there was, they won't have time to discuss it with you. A rude or self-pitying email from you – and they'll have a very good reason to never use your work. Strive to be a writer who's trouble-free to work with.

Relax!

Start again fast, seethe later – this is probably my best strategy! Make an appointment with yourself to seethe at about 8pm, let's say. Just postpone the bitterness until then. Meanwhile, write and perhaps send out another article, or the same one re-vamped. When 8pm comes around, you might find the urge to be bitter about the rejection has even left you.

See your rejection as a learning aid. Are there a couple of tweaks you could make to the piece before you send it out again? Re-read carefully. There could well be a change or two you can try . . . then submit it to a different magazine.

Try not to compare yourself to other writers who always seem to have success. Don't assume they have never experienced rejection. Of course they have. Writers don't always tell the truth! The friend who's constantly boasting about her success is probably as nervous as you are when she submits . . . because she's had rejections she doesn't admit to.

Celebrate what you have written, not your rejection! Look at cuttings from the past and reassure yourself that you have actually been published! Keep a 'boasting' book of nice emails from editors and letters from readers or people you've interviewed. If you've never been published, that's fine – it's just a matter of time. Instead, celebrate you and your writing talent.

Star turn?

Remind yourself that one magazine's rejection is another magazine's star turn.

Good goals

A marvellous way to defeat rejection blues is to make magazine writing goal lists. It's important to make your goals, though big, always achievable. Give yourself enough time to do the preparation work.

Work out how long it might take you to write a short story, prepare for a writing holiday, research a series of articles, draft a couple of columns. The initial preparation work is important – that can't be done by magic. It wouldn't be realistic to have as your goal a short story that you haven't even written, published next week! Yet if you do the preparation work and set the goal in detail, you could be surprised with the results.

If you want to know more about this strategy, I recommend you invest in a copy of *Write It Down, Make It Happen!* by Henriette Anne Klauser (Simon & Schuster, £10). Though not specifically about writing goals, it tells you more about this form of goal-setting and offers many fascinating exercises.

Mood-lifting goals

Look at your goal list on a rejection day and you'll find your negative thoughts will turn into ideas for things you could write. Your mood will lift.

It's essential to keep that goals journal in your writing notebook. Your notebook, in a way, is a part of you – it should have become vital. Keep writing in it every day. So buy a nice one – maybe with a pretty cover, spiral bound, or with an artwork cover you find inspiring.

Choose at least one from this list of suggested weekly goals:

- To write every day for at least ten minutes in my notebook.

- To observe scenes as I go about my daily life – and to write them up as soon as I can.

- To read a chapter of a how-to book on writing, or a chapter of a writing course.

- To clip articles and snippets which interest me from the newspapers and magazines I read.

- To send out a fresh article the same day I get a rejection.

- When I read a novel, to make a few comments about it in my notebook.

Monthly and annual goals

Here are some bigger goals for monthly aims:

- Make notes for a short story – and structure the beginning, middle and an end.

- Take the details of a writing competition, and begin notes for my entry – which I will send in good time.

Annual goals might be:

- Have a writing holiday, here or abroad.

- Join a writers' group locally.

- Book tickets for a literary festival.

Be rejected – then produce

If you are finding the rejection unbearable – and none of my tips seem to help change your state – think about a short achievable course or project you might do. It might be a two-hour workshop in yoga or autumn cookery, or a beginner's language course at a local college. It means getting out of the house and away from your desk, and thinking about something else – and that's a start!

It may be that disappointment and rejection have got you seriously down. It could be to do with your writing or with something else – but whatever it is might drain your vitality and energy for writing.

You can replace the 'musts' with more rational thinking. 'I must not be rejected ever' could be replaced with, 'I would much prefer not to be rejected, but if I am, I can take it, because there are no guarantees in life!'

Use self-reaffirmation more often and consciously:

- 'I tried my best with my article; being rejected does not mean I am no good.'
- 'My style did not match their requirements or preferences this time. Yes, I'd prefer not to have the piece rejected, but I can take it!'

Don't forget . . . it's not you that's been rejected – it's just that your work did not suit their needs at that time.

Most writers have more rejections than acceptances. Actors have the same problem – most of them spend most of their lives not working, at least not as actors. But they don't look on this as rejection. When they are working, the world sits down to watch them – just as when you sell an article, you have thousands of readers.

If you want to maintain a writing career, the one thing you need to be in control of is your emotions. Writing is reflection. If all your reflection is negative, it will be hard for you to create – you'll be too depressed!

Easier to say than do, I know.

'Celebrate what you have written, not your rejection! Look at cuttings from the past and reassure yourself that you have actually been published! Keep a 'boasting' book of nice emails from editors and letters from readers or people you've interviewed.'

Keep writing

Success is a matter of continuously hard work. Try to develop the ability to work hard continuously, not in fits and starts. This may sound harsh, but it isn't. Even if you only have an hour or two to spend writing each day, you can make that time one of constructive work, not mind-wandering.

If you can build up this writing stamina – and you can! – rejections will no longer have their disastrous effect.

'A marvellous way to defeat rejection blues is to make goal lists. Make a list of magazine writing goals. It's important to make your goals, though big, always achievable. Give yourself enough time to do the preparation work. Work out how long it might take you to write a short story, prepare for a writing holiday, research a series of articles, draft a couple of columns.'

Summing Up

'Most writers have more rejections than acceptances. Actors have the same problem – most spend most of their lives not working, at least not as actors. But they don't look on this as rejection. When they are working, the world sits down to watch them – just as when you sell an article, you have thousands of readers.'

- Don't despair when you have a rejection. Remember . . . one magazine's rejection can be another's star turn!
- Choose something pleasurable to do on a rejection day.
- Make writing goals to offset rejection blues.
- Keep a 'boasting book' of your praise mail.
- Keep a writing notebook to build up your writing stamina.

Chapter Ten

Keep Going!

What you need to do now is maintain your now-found confidence. You want to achieve those writing goals, and not to let setbacks get you down. This final section offers practical and inspirational aids to help you do just that.

You'll keep that confidence high by doing all you can to market yourself and your work, you will enjoy and develop the discipline of writing at home; and you'll get the habit of keeping an eye on the markets you're aiming for. You can pick up new markets – these are areas that might interest you.

How to be a magazine columnist

If you've had success with a couple of articles on the same theme – let's say student life or running a B&B – you might be able to identify a slot for a regular column.

Scour your selected magazines carefully – can you see a column there? If it's a magazine about gardening – or parenting, or teaching – can you think of opinions or advice you can offer? Witty reflections on your life as a new mum or retiree? A column about your life as an aspiring writer?

You should draft out two sample columns and attach them to your letter explaining the column's approach or slant, together with that picture of you and brief but engaging biography details.

Handling Q&A columns

If you have special knowledge of any topic – be it window sill gardening or DIY – offer a magazine a Q&A (Question and Answer) column. Readers love them! Five questions and answers will do. Keep them short, pithy . . . and informative.

My Q&A column

I do one for *Writing Magazine* – answering all kinds of questions from beginner writers on every aspect of the craft. That's because writing has always been my niche subject. I have also ghosted magazine Q&As about antiques, property, and travel in Greece. It involves getting the information from experts and customising it to fit the styles of the different magazines.

How about you? You may have special knowledge of travel, parenting, cleaning, cookery, computers, nursing, hairdressing. You don't have to be a world expert!

A top notch local cleaner who can write could easily do an entertaining and informative column on cleaning for a women's magazine. When you trawl through the glossies, you'll see that house cleaning and hygiene has become very topical – we all want short cuts to squeaky clean, germ-free homes. Look out for these simple but topical angles.

Celebrity writing

Interviewing a celebrity is often the Holy Grail for freelance magazine writers. It's easier than you think. Always have certain magazines in mind for your interview. For example, you could interview a celeb for both *My Weekly* and *The Daily Mail's You* magazine – you'll need different versions and a different style for each. The trick is to obtain enough quotes and information for two different versions of your interview.

Start with local celebs – who lives in your area? Where I live, we have Van Morrison, John Cleese, Nicolas Cage, Jilly Cooper and Joanna Trollope. There could be more I haven't found out about. I'm not saying that celebs will drop everything at your request – but if they live locally (and provided, usually, that they have something to 'sell' such as a new book, CD or film) they may be kind.

You can pitch a request to a celebrity by finding out the contact details of their agents, publishers or record label and writing to them. You should mention the magazine you are targeting. If you want to avoid saying this will be on spec, say, 'I am researching a feature on XXX for *Yours* magazine.'

It might be that they'd consent to an interview by email. Not ideal, but if you make your questions original enough – and do plenty of research on them so you don't have to waste time asking the nuts and bolts questions – you can create a good piece.

Be brave!

If you are lucky enough to meet a celebrity – maybe one attending a local event – pluck up your courage and approach them. It may seem as though you are barging in, but they are hardly likely to approach you! Politely say you are a magazine writer, and could they spare half an hour for an interview? If you are really lucky (and they are bored with the event!) they might give you an interview there and then. Have your questions ready. Carry your notebook, pens and camera at all times.

They might suggest a meeting at a later date, so make sure you get contact details from them. And secure that biographical material first – you don't want to waste precious minutes of an interview finding out where they were born and which schools they went to. Their agent or publisher should be able to supply these details, or it might be on their websites. See chapter 3 for more on questions to ask celebs!

Ignore this

Ignore, more or less, the PR handout that's dished out for celebs. There might be some useful basic information in it, but there'll also be a Niagara of gushing hyperbole. Note the useful details and bin the rest.

Recycle it!

Selling your work more than once is something that seems to make many freelance or hobby writers nervous. There's no need to be. As we've said, it's legal! It's your work and you are free to revamp it with a new angle, thus increasing your revenue and your profile.

How do you get those new angles? There's only one way – by being curious. You need to ask questions. And then you need to ask follow-up questions. You need to get the detail. You need to wring as much out of your interviewees and subjects as possible. That way you'll have content unused and left over for a second market.

Take this as an example. You're asking an interviewee to name their favourite holiday destination, and the short reply is, 'Italy'.

Keep probing

That's not enough. Continue your probing with these sorts of questions:

* Why Italy?
* Which part of Italy?
* How many times have you visited?
* Are you learning Italian?
* What's your favourite Italian meal?
* What's the journey in Italy you would most like to make?
* What Italian destination do you suggest for the first-time visitor?
* Do you have a favourite book or film about Italy?

All you have to do is ask – if you don't ask, you don't get.

Recycling shouldn't be an afterthought. Kick off with the intention of recycling it. Don't sell just a single feature on a topic. Check how many more magazines or newspapers might be interested – try your *Writers' & Artists' Yearbook* for this – or do some Internet research.

There are primary and secondary markets for all features. I've described one – here's another. Let's say you are doing a piece on a holiday hotel which is very child-friendly, having in-house nannies. You could do this first for a magazine about babies. But if you rewrite it with more about you as a mum relaxing, it could be right for *Practical Parenting*. And if you rework it, with more on the nannies and the service they offer (and the jobs for nannies in the travel arena) you could submit to *The Lady*, which has captured the market in jobs for nannies.

Six tips for recycling magazine features:

1. Change the introduction – make a third person intro into one that begins with a quote. Instead of 'The new route to Lille is expected to attract thousands of people to this pretty French market town', try 'I'll admit it – I've never been that keen on France. Yet my weekend in Lille was surprisingly pleasant'.

2. Change the ending.

3. Find a panel, box or sidebar which reuses some of your original material in a new way – change opinions into tips and general advice into dos and don'ts.

4. Start your piece earlier or later – rather than your first meal there, begin with the last one. You instantly freshen up your story.

5. Change adjectives to change the piece. If you've used adjectives such as sun-drenched . . . primitive . . . celebrated . . . remarkable, substitute scorching . . . basic . . . renowned . . . exemplary. Go through your piece inserting new adjectives for old.

6. Don't use up all of your facts and quotes in one piece – save some for recycling. That way each separate piece has the vital 'something different'. A new picture also adds a new angle – take, or get, a selection of pictures of your subject if you can.

> 'Selling your work more than once is something that seems to make many freelance or hobby writers nervous. There's no need to be.'

Enhance sales

Here are some more ways in which to build up your sales and foster relationships with magazine editors:

- If you meet an editor and have an encouraging conversation, follow this up with an email or letter instead of a telephone call.

- Try to reply to emails and telephone messages within 24 hours, and expect to pick up more work. The best way to do this is to timetable a half hour at the same time every evening. Or, if it suits you, the first hour of your working day.

- When you send a completed commissioned piece to an editor, accompany it with a separate document listing three new ideas you think would interest the journal for which you are writing.

Write in style

When you write at home, you want to feel comfortable, but not sloppy. It's important to feel good about yourself. How you feel about yourself all through the day adds up to a total feeling – you want it to be a positive one.

Simple soft trousers and T-shirts are good, and you might want to have a few outfits which become your 'writing uniform'. Keep a smart outfit for when you go out to do interviews.

Keep your confidence high!

This means being able to deal with rejection, and being able to deal with no response at all! All journals are poor at acknowledging submissions now. They will hang on to articles for months and months – let them without pestering. There's always a possibility that a slot will open up suddenly, perhaps because another writer has let the editor down. When that happens, your copy is there, ready to fill the gap. Always have new work on the go.

Compete!

So many talented writers give up. The secret of success is often not talent or even genius, but sheer persistence and dedication. 'The art of writing,' George Bernard Shaw warned, 'is 10% inspiration and 90% perspiration.' The stamina to write day after day even when there are no immediate rewards – that's the thing.

One way to gear up for this is to enter as many writing competitions as you can manage: How often do you think about entering a writing competition – and then not do it? You'll find your happiness level as a writer increases just by completing a short story or article and posting it off – it's very satisfying, and very good for building up your writing skills.

Decide to enter, make a timetable, and settle down for a regular daily or weekly writing sessions.

Outline your story first, then get it written. Some magazine writers try to do a short story a month, or every three months, to enter in competitions. Magazines such as *Woman&Home* and *Good Housekeeping* run competitions and *Writing* magazine has short story comps in every issue, plus an annual award for freelance articles.

Rules of competing

※ Read the rules of the competition carefully – there may be restrictions about age and where you live.

※ Some competitions don't accept emailed entries, others prefer them.

※ Submit your entry in plenty of time.

※ Keeping to the word count is vital – exceed it at your peril!

Successful? Tell the world

Spread the word when you get articles and short stories published. Let your local radio station, magazines and newspapers know. It might be that you could fill a slot by doing a radio talk on the same subject; local magazines like to highlight success by local writers.

Don't forget that photo of you. Always say you are available for interview in person or by phone. When I used to be a royalty correspondent for British and Australian magazines, I had phone calls asking for my views on royal this and royal that. I always made time for them. You'll be quoted as an expert on the topic – it could be anything from bringing up twins to marathon running.

Summing Up

- Enter writing competitions.

- Look around your area for local celebrities to interview.

- Identify slots for columns or Q&A features on topics you are passionate about or have a special interest in.

- Don't let rejections get you down – all writers have them!

- Recycle your articles.

- Spread the word when you get your work published.

'Try to reply to emails and telephone messages within 24 hours, and expect to pick up more work. The best way to do this is to timetable a half-hour at the same time every evening. Or, if it suits you, the first hour of your working day.'

FAQs

Should I have an agent?

Not worth it when you're a beginner – or even, sometimes, an established writer. Agents want at least a 10% cut of what can be quite modest fees.

If I have a feature published, can I send it to other magazines?

You can't send identical work to different titles. What you can do is use the content and change the form of words, adding new quotes and a new intro.

If I win a short story competition, can I submit the same story to a magazine?

It depends on the rules of the competition. If the rules allow, then yes. It's unlikely that the circulation of a large magazine would be affected by the reach of a small short story competition.

Is it worth joining an online database to advertise my writing skills?

Yes – especially if you have niche skills that you can promote. Sign up free to www.responsesource.com and your details go out to thousands of PRs and other media companies.

Can I start a blog or set up a website for free?

Yes – try www.blogger.com

'You'll find your happiness level as a writer increases just by completing a short story or article and posting it off – it's very satisfying, and very good for building up your writing skills.'

How long should I wait for a reply to a submission?

It could be a long time, maybe up to six months or even longer. Unsolicited submissions might not get a response.

Is it best to telephone an editor or email?

Email always!

If a rejection from a magazine highlights some improvements I could make, should I send the revised feature back to that magazine?

Try a new outlet. It's encouraging that they've indicated improvement gaps.

What is meant by a 'colour' piece?

This is an article which describes the setting and atmosphere of a special or unusual event – a royal wedding, a football cup final, or a funeral.

What's a how-to article?

Just what it says – a feature which tells the reader how to do something. It could be making meringues, organising a hen party, or making the most of the first year at college. Include tips and hints, box outs, dos and don'ts.

Do I hold copyright of everything I write and sell?

In theory, yes. But newspapers and magazines are increasingly asking for the world copyright of the articles they buy from freelance writers – sometimes for a specified number of years. It is usually spelt out in the contracts they send to freelancers. This does not preclude you from reusing your content – in a refreshed and revamped form.

Book List

Write It Down, Make It Happen
By Henriette Anne Klauser, Simon and Schuster, London 2001.
By recording your thoughts and desires on paper, you set in motion the wheels that take you to your goal. Try this book – and try the exercises – if writing for magazines is your aim.

On Writing
By Stephen King, New English Library, London 2000.
A personal voyage through the books and films which inspired this hugely successful writer. It's the book he wrote as soon as he could sit up after a road accident which required six operations to save his life.

Plotting and Writing Suspense Fiction
By Patricia Highsmith, St Martin's Press, New York 1966.
Highsmith shows how to develop an idea into a suspense short story – an ideal how-to for the beginner writer.

Writing Down the Bones
By Natalie Goldberg, Shambhala, London and Boston 1986.
Freeing the writer within. Good to get your notebook going.

The Magazines Handbook
By Jenny McKay, Routledge, London 2000.
Advice on starting out in the freelance industry, practical aspects of magazines, guide to all the skills needed If you want to pursue a career in magazine writing.

The Elements of Style
By Strunk and White, Macmillan, 1935
Still unrivalled simple guide to the craft of excellent writing.

Writers' & Artists' Yearbook
By A & C Black, London
www.writersandarrtists.co.uk

Useful magazines

Writers' Forum

www.writers-forum.com
Inspiring how-to articles on writing, plus competitions.

Writing Magazine (now combined with Writers' News)

Tel: 0113 200 2929
www.writersnews.co.uk
Competitions, articles on every aspect of writing short stories, as well as marketing – plus news of likely magazine markets for writers.

Courses

The Arvon Foundation

60 Farringdon Road, London, EC1R 3GA
Tel: 0207 3242554
www.arvonfoundation
Wide range of residential courses on magazine and short story writing at country houses in England and Scotland. Grants available.

National Union of Journalists (NUJ)

www.nujtraining.org.uk
The NUJ runs courses which help develop skills and confidence for start-up freelance journalists, including magazine writers.

Swanwick, The Writers' Summer School

www.wss.org.uk
Dozens of courses for beginner short story and magazine article writers at this famous summer school established more than 60 years ago.

Travellers' Tales

92 Hillfield Road London NW6 1QA

www.travellerstales.org
Masterclass and first-timer courses for magazine travel writers in London and abroad.

Ty Newydd Writers' Centre

Ty Newydd, Llanystumdwy, Criccieth, Gwynedd, LL52 OLW
Tel: 01766 522811
www.tynewydd.org
Look on their website for courses on short story magazine writing.

Winchester Writers' Conference and Bookfair

University of Winchester, Winchester, Hants
www.writersconference.co.uk
This festival of writing offers 22 workshops, 60 talks and 500 one-to-ones to help writers harness their creative talents and their editing and marketing skills. There are 17 writing competitions and 70 prizes. Held annually at the end of June.

Writers' Retreat

St Cuthman's

Cowfield Road, Coolham, West Sussex RH13 8QL
www.stcuthmans.com
Grappling with writers' block or longing for peace to work on your short stories and articles? This Roman Catholic retreat house can offer writers a tranquil setting . . . simple yet comfortable rooms and fresh home-cooked food. There are daily (non-obligatory) prayers.

Writing holidays abroad

Skyros

www.skyros.com

Hard copy
Copy supplied on paper rather than by email.

Head
The 'title' or headline which attracts the reader to the article.

Intro
The first paragraph of the feature. Sometimes called the nose.

Pull quote
A sentence extracted from the article and set in contrasting type. A visual device to break up the text.

Sell
A paragraph appearing below or alongside the headline which explains what the article is about. Also known as the standfirst.

Stet
Literal translation of the Latin for 'let it stand'. It means that a marked correction has been made in error – ignore it.

Wordcount
Total number of words required for a feature.

Need · 2 · Know

Available Titles Include ...

Publishing Poetry The Essential Guide
ISBN 978-1-86144-113-3 £9.99

Writing Poetry The Essential Guide
ISBN 978-1-86144-112-6 £9.99

Writing Non-Fiction Books The Essential Guide
ISBN 978-1-86144-114-0 £9.99

Book Proposals The Essential Guide
ISBN 978-1-86144-118-8 £9.99

Writing Dialogue The Essential Guide
ISBN 978-1-86144-119-5 £9.99

Creating Fictional Characters The Essential Guide
ISBN 978-1-86144-120-1 £9.99

Writing Romantic Fiction The Essential Guide
ISBN 978-1-86144-121-8 £9.99

Pilates The Essential Guide
ISBN 978-1-86144-097-6 £9.99

Surfing The Essential Guide
ISBN 978-1-86144-106-5 £9.99

Gardening A Beginner's Guide
ISBN 978-1-86144-100-3 £9.99

Going Green The Essential Guide
ISBN 978-1-86144-089-1 £9.99

Food for Health The Essential Guide
ISBN 978-1-86144-095-2 £9.99

Vegan Cookbook The Essential Guide
ISBN 978-1-86144-123-2 £9.99

Walking A Beginner's Guide
ISBN 978-1-86144-101-0 £9.99

View the full range at **www.need2knowbooks.co.uk**. To order our titles call **01733 898103**, email **sales@n2kbooks.com** or visit the website. Selected ebooks available online.

Need - 2 - Know, Remus House, Coltsfoot Drive, Peterborough, PE2 9BF